D0193027

The Pocket Muse

The Pocket Muse

ideas &
inspirations
for writing

Monica Wood

WRITER'S DIGEST BOOKS
Cincinnati, Ohio
www.writersdigest.com

Visit our Web site at www.writersdigest.com for information on more resources for writers.

To receive a free weekly e-mail newsletter delivering tips and updates about writing and about Writer's Digest products, register directly at our Web site at http://newsletters.fwpublications.com.

06 05 04 03 02   5 4 3 2 1

Library of Congress Cataloging-in-Publication Data
Wood, Monica
The pocket muse: ideas and inspirations for writing/ by Monica Wood.
p. cm.
ISBN 1-58297-142-0 (alk.paper)
1. Authorship. I. Title.

PN147.W58 2001
808'.02–dc21
2001056755
CIP

Edited by Jack Heffron and Meg Leder
Designed by Lisa Buchanan
Cover photography by © Digital Vision
Page makeup by Matthew DeRhodes
Production coordinated by Kristen D. Heller
Author photo by Dan Abbott

Photographs on pages 16, 17, 33, 63, 87, 90, 129, 153, 163, 175, and 196 by Brian Schroeder.
Photographs on pages 51, 83, 156, and 182 by Ron Ellis, Sr.
Photograph on page 114 courtesy of Ron Ellis, Sr.
Photographs on pages 60, 123, 136. 146, 151, 200 and 216 by Bob Thompson.
Photograph on page 96 by Lisa Buchanan.
Photograph on page 71 and 106 by Kelly Shields.
Photograph on page 166 by Daniel Cosner.

Acknowledgments

I am gladly indebted to my editor, Jack Heffron, for his careful pen and abiding good humor. I also thank Bob Thompson for giving me photographs so eye-catching that some of these pages seemed to write themselves. And thank you, Ron Ellis, Sr., who at age ninety-three still has great memories—and, lucky for me, photographs—of his years as zoo director at the Prospect Park Zoo in Brooklyn, New York.

About the Author

Monica Wood is the author of two novels, *My Only Story* (Chronicle, 2000; Ballantine, 2001) and *Secret Language* (Faber and Faber, 1993; Ballantine, 2002), and a book of connected short stories entitled *Ernie's Ark* (Chronicle, 2002; Ballantine 2003). She is also the author of *Description*, from the Writer's Digest Elements of Fiction series, and several guides to contemporary literature in the high school classroom. Her short stories have been widely published and anthologized.

Fifteen years ago,

when I was thirty-two years old, I quit my day job. I was a high school guidance counselor, and my job was hard, requiring equal parts objectivity and compassion to solve an ever-changing onslaught of problems. It also brought me into daily contact with people—mostly teenagers, but also teachers, parents, social workers, community leaders, sometimes even the police. The job was busy, harrying, rewarding, multifaceted. I loved it. And I quit.

I wanted to write, needed to write, until eventually the tension between my profession and my vocation became such that I had to let one of them go. Most writers, as much as they might want to do the same, can't. I was lucky to be young and relatively unencumbered, and to have a spouse willing to make the financial sacrifice with me—a sacrifice that is ongoing even for seemingly successful writers. Despite the risks, the rewards seemed worth the leap, so I leapt.

For two years I lived what most people would consider the ideal writing life. It wasn't ideal, however, because nothing is. Although temperamentally suited to the writing trade—stubborn, disciplined, inclined toward solitude—I felt unexpectedly lonely in my new incarnation. I found myself yearning for the job I'd left: the daily hum, the voices around me, the press of real life. I had everything a writer could want—support, time, and a room of my own—and ran smack into the writer's paradox: You can't write without living fully, and you can't live fully and still find time to write.

Writers get past this paradox in various ways—they work as lounge singers, they write in bus terminals, they hire nannies and throw lots of parties, they become the town crank. I turned to teaching—not full-time, and not year-round, but enough to engage me in the lives of people outside my own domestic sphere. (It also kept my social skills from eroding completely.)

Teaching reminds me of what I know and love about writing. It introduces me to a fascinating cross section of the world. In one workshop alone I met a college student, an advertising director, and an eighty-eight-year-old retired bus driver. I've gotten to know nurse practitioners, lobstermen, psychiatrists, head waiters, new mothers, dog groomers, family doctors. I believe they come to me not only to improve their skills but to seek a writing life. And because my own writing life has taken several forms, I believe I can help them.

Every writer—whether beginner or veteran, full-time or crunch-time—faces the same old problems. Problems of time management, discipline, inspiration, and motivation. Not to mention frustration, despair, and the throat-closing terror of the blank page. Oh, and joy—the exploding, dopey joy of getting the words down right—that, too, visits us all. This book will, I hope, enrich the joyful days and prevent the days of head-banging from wrecking your spirit.

The Pocket Muse can be read randomly, each page containing something to jump-start a writing session, inspire confidence, or strengthen your resolve. It can also be read chronologically, as a course in getting your writing life together. On some pages you get a pat on the head, on others a kick in the seat. Every single page contains my hope to inspire, cajole, goad, shove, or otherwise lead you into a fully lived writing life marked by good work, perseverance, connection, and satisfaction.

These pages include writing prompts and exercises, quotations (fresh ones) from a variety of writers, mini-lessons on technique, strategies for battling writer's block, suggestions (and orders) for maintaining your writing life, cautionary tales from the book world, and a few laughs. The black-and-white photographs throughout intensify the directions or advice on the page, but they can also be used alone as idea-starters. A few of them are accompanied by a single word or phrase to spark the imagination. You will also find "horoscopes" sprinkled throughout the book, which you can use as a way to imagine new paths for both major and minor characters, whether you're writing fiction, poetry, or nonfiction. Feel free to play with the pages, combining prompts, imagining relationships between unrelated photographs, applying the technical tip on one page directly to the exercise on another. I'm a firm believer that the writing life should contain more light than darkness, and I hope this book will help you write toward light.

I wrote this book with two audiences in mind. One, my writer friends, who, like me, suffer from occasional failures of confidence, imagination, courage; most of the advice herein derives from pep talks to myself. Two, my students—the ones who dress toddlers every morning, the ones who commute five hours a day, the ones filling their final years with memory, the ones fresh out of school and trying to find their voice. It is to these students, who seek a writing life even when luck and circumstance fail them, that I dedicate this book.

What are you waiting for?
If not now, when?

Write about someone who is pretending to be someone or something that he is not.

Write about a noise—
or a silence—
that won't go away.

In *Making Shapely Fiction*, the witty and wonderful Jerome Stern cautions against writing the "bathtub story." A bathtub story opens with the protagonist taking a bath (or occupying a similar confined space). During this bath, the protagonist thinks of, ruminates upon, wonders about, and analyzes the past, present, and future, but *he never gets out of the bathtub.*

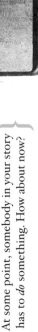

At some point, somebody in your story has to *do* something. How about now?

A Tip on Style

When revising your work, don't forget to examine your modifiers.
Are your adverbs doing too much work, shoring up weak verbs?
Would a more muscular verb render the adverb unnecessary?

Gordon walked quickly across the yard.

Depending on Gordon's state of mind, he could be *lurching,
hurrying, quick-stepping,* or *fleeing.*

DeeDee danced awkwardly to the music.

The precise nature of DeeDee's crummy dancing might be clearer if you replace *danced awkwardly* with *twitched, shuddered,*
or *hopscotched.*

Writing happens sentence by sentence. The joy of creative
expression lies in finding not a way, but *the way*—the only way—
to say what you mean.

Write about a less-than-remarkable aspect of your life.

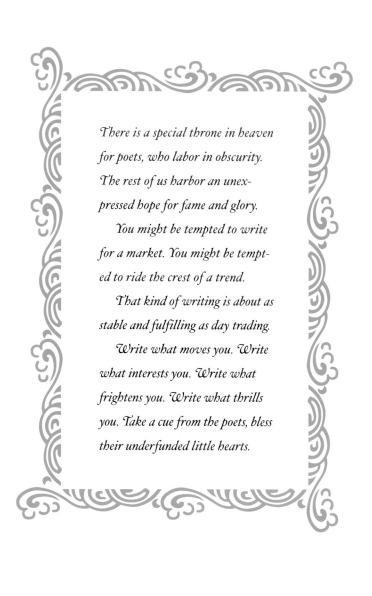

There is a special throne in heaven for poets, who labor in obscurity. The rest of us harbor an unexpressed hope for fame and glory.

You might be tempted to write for a market. You might be tempted to ride the crest of a trend.

That kind of writing is about as stable and fulfilling as day trading.

Write what moves you. Write what interests you. Write what frightens you. Write what thrills you. Take a cue from the poets, bless their underfunded little hearts.

Make two lists:

1. Everything you know about your subject	2. Everything you want to know about your subject

Use the following verbs in any way you wish:

racket snug green spoon boggle snake

They're not all verbs, you say?
Jeremy is racketing across the lawn as we speak!
Can you hear earthworms snugging out of the
ground as the sun greens the trees?

Verbs are sometimes a matter of opinion.

Who is the TALLEST person you know?

THE LOUDEST?

The homeliest?

`The crankiest?`

The meekest?

*People at the bitter end of
any continuum invite trouble.
Begin with an extreme and see what happens.*

"It all means little, all the painting, sculpture, drawing, writing . . . it all has its place and nothing more. An attempt is everything. How marvelous!"

—Alberto Giacometti

{ Make the attempt. }

A Revision Tool for the Truly Desperate

Have a friend make ten random marks in the margin of your manuscript. Cut the manuscript into pieces, according to this random design. (You won't believe how good this feels!)

Now, mix up the pieces and tape the manuscript back together. Read it. It won't make much sense, of course, especially as you read the newly conjoined thoughts that occur at the random seams.

What happens? Something will dawn on you. Some configuration of words that did not appear in the original will spawn a new idea, a different angle, a peek into your subconscious.

Routine Maintenance Schedule for the Writing Life

Once a week: Skip to the next part of whatever you're working on, no matter how stuck you feel.

Once a month: Write all day without talking to anybody.

Every three months: Send something out for publication, just to keep your hand in.

Every six months: Clean your workspace: Pitch obsolete files, lumpen drafts, rejection slips, leaky pens, old mail. Clear away the dross, and you'll be able to think more clearly.

Once a year: Take a chunk of time, whatever you can afford— three full days, minimum—and go someplace where your writing will not be disturbed except for eating and sleeping.

Today's horoscope:
COMPANY FROM OUT OF TOWN.
COULD MEAN TROUBLE.

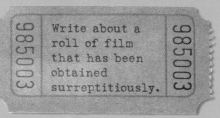

985003

Write about a
roll of film
that has been
obtained
surreptitiously.

985003

A Tip on Style

One way to enliven your prose is to avoid the use of the verb *to be*: am, are, is, was, were, etc. Very often you can trace a dull passage to the overuse of that pesky verb. Look at these two examples:

> When she finally emerged from the house, Mary was stunned. The sun was blinding, but the weather was cold. All around her were frozen trees that had broken off at their waists. Everything was both beautiful and awful.

Eliminating the verb *to be* forces you to think about your method of expression, often yielding a more poetic and precise passage:

> Mary emerged from the house, stunned by a blinding sun. The trees, broken off at their waists, lay over the yard, each naked branch encased in a sleeve of ice. The day felt both beautiful and awful.

Writer's Block?

If you have a dog or a cat, brush him.
Take a lot of time. Relax. Compose your
thoughts. Don't panic.

> *If you don't have a pet,*
> *find a kid and braid her hair.*

Choose ten random letters of the alphabet, and write them at the top of a blank page.

Example:

C W I T S N E M B R

Using words that begin with these letters, in the same order, write an opening sentence. These letters yielded the following sentences from one of my writing workshops:

> "Cindy's winning?" Ian teased, suddenly nervous. "Everett may be right."

> Carolyn's wristwatch, Ida's terriers, Susan's notebooks: Exposed memory bruised Robert.

> Catholics wormed into the Suburban, never expecting my brother's ruse.

> Certain women, instinctively tentative, seemed nervous entering Minnie's burgeoning ranch.

> Cool water is tempting. Splash! New, magical entries bring rewards.

Notes From the Book Tour

My friend Rich Kent once did a book signing in the old hometown. Though gratified by the turnout, he stumbled upon the inevitable moment in every writer's life: the familiar face, the expectant smile, the proffered book . . . the forgotten name.

"And how do you spell it?" Rich said, grasping for cover.

The fellow paused, then answered: "B-O-B."

For years now, I've been keeping what I call a "word notebook." It's a tiny spiral notebook with lined pages, six by four inches, in which I keep lists of words. Not phrases, not quotations, just words.

The notebook accompanies my reading; whenever I stumble upon a word I like, I transfer it to the notebook. Sometimes I record words I have to look up, but mostly I record common words that I haven't used in a while or words I simply love the sound of.

My word notebook travels with me from my reading area to my writing area. I use it on days when words come hard. Sometimes I check my notebook for a zesty word that can replace a dull one. Often, I'll combine words pulled from the notebook until a good sentence appears out of the mist. I also do word-association exercises with words taken from my notebook, allowing one good word to engender another until I hit upon a decent idea.

Today's entries:

sylph

rabble

fizzy

styptic

freckled

Today's the day. No more fooling around.

Set an egg timer for forty-five minutes, and don't get out of the chair until the timer dings. Even if you sit staring at the page the entire time, you're ingraining a habit.

Chickens and fraidy-cats may begin with five-minute segments.

I once took care of a friend's infant, a little girl named Grace, three mornings a week for about five months. Because I was writing my first novel at the time, I entered into these child-care duties with great trepidation, believing myself incapable of writing except at my own desk, in my own studio, on my own schedule, in absolute quiet.

The novel got finished, I believe now, not in spite of but because of my friend Grace, now ten years old. Notebook in hand, I wrote on the handle of the stroller as we walked through the neighborhood. Laptop in lap, I typed with my fingers while rocking her baby seat with my toes. I sang songs to her while waiting for something in the work to move. I used her (this will be the first her mother's heard of this) as a writing table, propping my notebook on her back as she lay, oblivious, across my lap.

Grace was a somber baby with serious eyes. Even a person with no imagination at all could see her possibilities as a Muse. This Muse said, "Walk me. Put my hat on. Take my hat off. Feed me. Change me. Sing. Pick me up. Put me down." All that activity was good for the work. We don't always need our solitude.

{ Train yourself to write anywhere. }

Write the following in the voice
of a fifty-two-year-old man:

I could have avoided
all that trouble if only
I had remembered to . . .

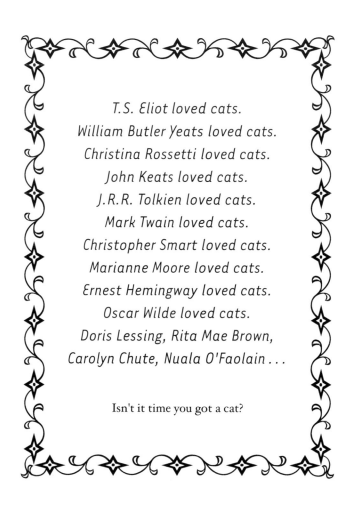

T.S. Eliot loved cats.
William Butler Yeats loved cats.
Christina Rossetti loved cats.
John Keats loved cats.
J.R.R. Tolkien loved cats.
Mark Twain loved cats.
Christopher Smart loved cats.
Marianne Moore loved cats.
Ernest Hemingway loved cats.
Oscar Wilde loved cats.
Doris Lessing, Rita Mae Brown,
Carolyn Chute, Nuala O'Faolain...

Isn't it time you got a cat?

Invent an Opposite

What is the opposite of a kiss?

What is the opposite of green?

What is the opposite of a train?

What is the opposite of cake?

What is the opposite of a fence?

Now, use both the thing and its
opposite in a story, poem, or essay.

Don't check your
e-mail today
until you've written
three pages.

a ringing phone

a sealed envelope

an unidentifiable sound

two men in orange sneakers

a rare bird

a broken clock

Add one of these ingredients to a scene or stanza that is not working in its present form.

If, after all your best efforts, the piece you're writing must be abandoned, do not despair. There is no such thing as wasted writing. Sometimes you must search and destroy, search and destroy, search and destroy before finding your true subject. Kiss those hard-earned pages good-bye—fondly, if you can manage it—and take out a beautiful, clean sheet. The new, marvelous thing you are about to write will emerge not despite those abandoned pages, but because of them.

A character arrives at work to find her chair missing. What happened to it?

Treat yourself to:

an expensive pen
a box of colorful paper clips
a fine, handmade notebook
a leather bookmark

{ Why shouldn't your tools be beautiful? }

Complication vs. Situation: A Primer

I once spent four miserable years on a version of a novel that had a great situation: a murder-suicide that left an orphaned child who was taken in by her aunts. My problem? I mistook *situation* for *complication*. A *situation,* however complicated, is self-contained. A *complication,* however simple, opens up, affording a path out. Excellent complications afford several paths out. In a short story, you take one path; in a novel you might take five.

Insufficient complication is a problem that crops up frequently in student work. Train yourself to know the difference before you go charging off to the inevitable dead end.

For example, one student story I seem to see over and again concerns the depressed character considering suicide. Even if the character is holding the gleaming gun to his sweaty forehead, this is not a complication. This is a situation. The situation might be tense and dramatic, but it is essentially self-contained; it offers the story no egress, no way out other than to circle back to the guy with the gun. He either pulls the trigger or he doesn't. He might tell the story of Fern, his ego-stompin', double-dealin', stone-hearted girlfriend, but we're still left with a guy and a gun and a big ho-hum.

If the student, a beginner, doesn't recognize the limitations here or refuses to acknowledge them, then she is consigned to many weeks (in my case, years, and I wasn't even a beginner) of futile tinkering with an immovable object.

So, how does one turn a situation into a complication, one that will engender the story's rising action and lead to a climax and a denouement that satisfies both writer and reader?

One starts adding, is what one does. Pile it on, baby, until something cracks.

What if the depressed person holding a gun to his head gets a phone call—a wrong number? Who might this wrong number be? What might this wrong number say? What if the wrong number is herself a person in trouble? What if the wrong number demands something of the depressed person? How does the depressed person solve this problem?

Bingo, we're writing again.

A good complication illuminates, thwarts, or alters the character's desire.

A good complication forces the character to act.

A good complication offers the story a point of departure.

A good complication raises the stakes.

A good complication thickens the plot.

The Bible is a magical repository for story
ideas. Every story is a metaphor with limitless
possibilities for retelling.

Place Lot's wife at a school
board meeting in Kansas.

Tempt Adam with a Corvette
rather than an apple.

Turn Job into a bus driver and
give him a test that even God
couldn't dream up.

My friend Alyson Hagy,
whose writing makes me swoon,
gave me the best writing advice I ever got:

You have to be willing
to write badly.

Fill in the blank:

When I first told
my family about
_____,
they didn't believe me.

What does your writing space look like? Is it set off from the maelstrom of your family life, or are the kids allowed to plunder and pillage at will? Is your writing space also the bill-paying spot, the mail storehouse, the hats-and-mittens repository?

Don't you deserve a room of your own? If not a room, then a desk? If not a desk, then a table? If not a table, then a TV tray? You don't have to live in a palace to claim a space.

Ingredients of a good writing space:

❶ The space should be separated from its immediate surroundings. A folding screen works if you don't have a wall. A potted plant works if you don't have a screen. A big pile of books might even work if you don't have a potted plant. You can engineer something that will prevent you from seeing the laundry basket, the unpaid bills, the television set. (I used to work at a rolltop desk whose back faced into the living room. It was an ugly setup. But when I was sitting at that desk, I could not see over the top, and I felt as if I'd entered a little room-within-a-room.)

❷ The space should be yours and yours alone. No other humans allowed in. Animals allowed as needed.

❸ The space should be used for creative endeavors and absolutely nothing else.

❹ The space should feel pleasant and contain a source of natural light.

❺ The space should be marked as yours by the decor: a favorite vase, a framed photo, a special charm or knick-knack. Put up a sign, a flag, a fence; pee on it if you have to. It's yours.

a fool's
paradise

WRITING CAN BE HARD
ON THE BODY.
DON'T FORGET TO GET UP
AND STRETCH, OFTEN!

WHILE YOU'RE STRETCHING,
SAY A PRAYER, RECITE
A POEM, HUM A SONG . . .
KEEP YOURSELF IN A
MEDITATIVE STATE.

A Tip on Style

Writing in the present tense requires extra attention to sentence structure. Try to vary the sentence structure so that the present tense recedes into the narrative. A string of simple declarative (subject-verb-object) sentences makes for a staccato feel that casts a neon light on your present-tense technique:

> Max walks into his office. It is too hot. Julie looks up suspiciously from her desk. The whole place takes on the feel of an interrogation. Even the lights seem brighter. He takes off his coat.

By combining sentences, attending to verbs, and altering sentence structure (for example, beginning with a phrase rather than a clause), you shed light on the story rather than the technique:

> Walking into the sweltering office, Max finds Julie eyeing him from her desk. Before he can manage to shed his coat, the place takes on the feel of an interrogation. Even the lights seem brighter.

Do something with these words:

vale

simper

fling

cranberry

kiosk

winsome

prey

quacky

I once heard a college student in Waterville, Maine, ask visiting writer Ron Carlson how one knows if one is really a writer. Ever the showman, Carlson delivered an entertaining riff about the distractions writers put in their own way, all day, all the time: leaving the room to get coffee, check the mail, get coffee, walk the dogs, go to the bathroom, get coffee, look something up, get coffee. Then, dead serious, he summed up the whole enterprise in a line I have never forgotten: "The writer is the one who stays in the room."

{ Be the one who stays in the room. }

Write about the last time you got your wish.

Write about the first time you got your wish.

If you have never gotten your wish, write about that.

A Tip on Structure

Most good stories, even unconventional ones,
contain these classic story elements:

Setup:	Three bears go for a walk while their porridge cools.
Complication:	Blonde perpetrator breaks in.
Rising Action:	Perp chows down, breaks a chair, gets some shut-eye.
Meanwhile:	Bears get home and survey the wreckage.
Climax:	Discovered in Baby Bear's bed, perp screams and flees.
Denouement:	Bears live happily ever after.

{ Does your story have a missing piece? }

Write about an appliance, a weapon, or a vehicle being put to a use for which it was not designed.

These hippos are called

Dodger and Betsey.

Your challenge is to figure out
how they got into the parking
lot of a Catholic school.

{ "Cleverness is not wisdom."
—Euripides }

Listen to your elders. There comes a point in every draft when you have to examine a turn of phrase—maybe your favorite one, the one that occasioned the entire piece. Be honest: Does the smarty-pants phrasing illuminate something at the heart of the work, or are you just being a show-off, a smart aleck, a writer's writer? Be careful with these beloved phrases—sometimes we can't tell the difference between cleverness and wisdom.

Here's an exercise my husband hates.

Go to a restaurant with somebody patient.

Pretend to be listening to him while you eat.

Meanwhile, grab a swatch of conversation

from Table A and another swatch from Table B.

Combine and enjoy.

Today's horoscope:

YOUR WISH BECOMES
SOMEBODY'S COMMAND.

Does your family have its own language? My elders, who came to Maine by way of Prince Edward Island, Canada, use lots of colorful phrases and expressions that I like to find space for in my prose. *Fearful* means "very," and *despisable* means "ill-tempered," as in "she's a fearful despisable child." (They weren't talking about me—I'm sure it was my sister!)

{ Do you have a piece of writing that could use an infusion of family dialect? }

As a reader and writer, I love encountering first sentences that

simultaneously summon the past and foreshadow the future.

Here are some of my favorite examples:

"All that day as she waited for her sister to come home, Maxine
remembered the goats."

—"Testimony," a short story by Jessica Treadway

"One night the baby died, and a few days later the mother, Mrs.
Silver, came to Belle's house and said, 'I want to talk to you.'"

—"Love Field," a short story by Lee Martin

"Although just barely—without *laudes*, without distinction, and
from an academy which is third-rate at best—Suzanne Kaplan's
son, Seth, has managed to graduate from prep school, and
Suzanne is having a party to celebrate."

—"Family Dancing," the title story from a collection by David Leavitt

"That night when he came to claim her, he stood on the short lawn before her house, his knees bent, his fists driven into his thighs, and bellowed her name with such passion that even the friends who surrounded him, who had come to support him, to drag her from the house, to murder her family if they had to, let the chains they carried go limp in their hands."

—*That Night*, a novel by Alice McDermott

"Since my attack last year, when I get off work at night one of my brothers is always waiting for me in our family car, the rusted boat, engine idling, double-parked on Halsted right outside Mizzi's, where I wait tables."

—"In the Land of Men," the title story from a collection by Antonya Nelson

"When Carnes got out of the hospital in Stockholm, we offered him the horn of his choice, the studio of his dreams, and luxurious support for as long as he stayed clean."

—*Tenorman*, a novella by David Huddle

Aren't these sentences magical? In each one, some provocative past event is being conjured just as a present event is about to begin. Try your hand at a few. The right sentence might spark an entire story.

Take a lesson.
In anything.
French. Ballroom dancing.
Beginning bird-watching.

Even if you hate the lesson, use it. Characters need
jobs and hobbies. Essays on new experiences, bad
or good, are fun to write. Poetry surely profits from
experiences outside your normal realm.

A character walks into the kitchen
at the end of the day. He finds
something on the kitchen table that
is not supposed to be there.

Every writer I know loves reference books. Allow yourself the unique pleasure of building a reference collection. Browsing through these books is pleasing, informative, and inspiring. Collect dictionaries, encyclopedias, books on craft, essays on writing—whatever interests you. No matter what the Internet has to offer in the way of quickie reference, there is no substitute for a soft chair and a big book.

At eye level, over the screen of my laptop, I find the following:

Word Court by Barbara Wallraff
Roget's Thesaurus in Dictionary Form
Novel & Short Story Writer's Market
Words Into Type
Writing Past Dark by Bonnie Friedman
The Oxford Companion to the English Language
The Macmillan Concise Encyclopedia
The Timetables of History by Bernard Grun
The King James Bible
Starting From Scratch: A Different Kind of Writers' Manual
   by Rita Mae Brown
The Writer's Idea Book by Jack Heffron
The New Fowler's Modern English Usage edited by R.W. Burchfield

Stuck? Draw a picture, even if you can't draw. Draw the place you're trying to describe. Draw the character who's eluding you. Something from your subconscious will appear on the page, I promise. Whatever it is will give you a place from which to resume writing.

Write about someone whose field of vision,

either literal or figurative, has narrowed

in the last six weeks.

At Christmastime one year,

I visited a house that had in the living room a stunning blue spruce with white ornaments. Just white, all up and down, with small, twinkly white lights. At first I thought, Oh, my, how beautiful, but after a little while, that tree started to depress me. It looked too much like a room furnishing. I prefer the garage sale method of tree trimming: red tinsel, ornaments from first-graders, red ball closeouts from Marden's, and one or two truly beautiful, maybe even valuable, shiny objects. And something on top that's been handed down over a few generations. The garage sale tree is a metaphor for the ideal writing life. That other tree is a metaphor for a frightened imagination.

{ If you don't risk being garish, you risk being bland. }

A Tip on Writing Dialogue

When writing dialogue, eliminate hellos and good-byes. Salutations usually gum up the works without adding a shred of character development or forward motion.

Dialogue from inexperienced writers often reads like this:

> "Hello."
> "Mitzi, is that you?"
> "Yes, it's me."
> "What do you want?"
> "Well, it's about Fluffy."

And so forth, paralyzing the story's momentum. When the phone rings, skip to the point:

> Igor picked up the phone. It was Mitzi, bent on delivering the latest installment of Fluffy's confinement.
> "She's doing that weird drooly thing again," she said. "I need you to pick up some of her special food."

Similarly, when it's time to hang up, ditch the farewells and disconnect:

> "There's nothing wrong with that stupid lizard that a healthy dose of neglect won't cure," Igor said.
> "Are you going to start on her? Don't you even think about starting on her."
> They went on like this for another ten minutes, until Igor hung up, hauled on his coat, and headed to the pet store.

Writers require, maybe even crave, connection with all the stages of life. We need old people, children, peers, teenagers, people we envy, people we pity, the whole human spectrum.

How many people do you talk to on a regular basis? Is it time to expand your world a bit? Take a kid to a ball game. Chat with the local librarian. Ask the counter girl at the 7-Eleven where she's from. Say hello to that neighbor you've never met.

If you say you're a writer, they'll tell you a story.

Write about a simple board game that
turns its players into pie-eyed cutthroats.

I call this exercise "color coding."
First, identify the area you wish to address:

Plot?

Theme?

Language/style?

Ratio of analysis to incident?

Dialogue vs. narrative?

Reflection vs. action?

Next, apply highlighters in different colors
to diagnose possible problems:

Example 1: Personal essay

Reflection vs. action: Highlight all the action in green, all the reflection in pink.

If you end up with mostly pink (reflection), you're probably preaching rather than evoking. The plight of the family farmer is indeed a pity; now show us the broken fences and dead cows.

If the piece has lots of green (action) and almost no pink (reflection), you're probably telling an anecdote with no thematic implications. The hike across Siberia was interesting, but what did it mean to you?

Example 2: Short fiction

Plot threads: Highlight everything about the broken marriage in yellow, everything about the construction project in green, everything about the kid's school problems in blue.

A scattershot of blue amidst oceans of yellow and green might indicate a plot thread that hasn't earned a place in the story.

Lots of one color early on, then nothing, means you've dropped the ball on that plot thread.

Lots of one color at the end probably reveals a last-minute complication that you haven't prepared the reader for.

Example 3: Poem

Language/style: Highlight abstract language ("she loved him/with heart and soul") in pink; concrete language ("she counted his eyelashes/numbered the knobs of his spine") in orange.

Too much pink (abstract)—Is the poem lazy, clichéd, too generalized to imply very much?

Too much orange (concrete)—There's no such thing as too much orange.

Looking at a piece graphically is enlightening, humbling, and entertaining.

Write about a person whose reputation
rests on the appearance of an
inanimate object.

"'Tweet, tweet.' That's the opinion of David, poet, friend, and guest from Philadelphia. By it, he means many things. Among the most obvious: that birdwatching is merely insipid and that by chasing after birds, I had forfeited the seriousness the poet owes the world. David thinks himself tough, unillusioned. For him, the primary obligation of poets is to engage the ugly front of the reality of our time."

—poet Leonard Nathan, in
Diary of a Left-Handed Birdwatcher

{ When engaging the ugly front of reality, don't neglect the beauty in the back. }

Top five day jobs for writers, based
on an informal and deeply flawed poll:

❶ Security guard
❷ Parrot trainer
❸ Bounty hunter
❹ Greeter at Wal-Mart
❺ Neurosurgeon

In other words, find something that
nets you either lots of material or lots
of time.

What have you been reading lately? Most writers are obsessive readers.

Of course they are: Wide and indiscriminate reading is part of the job. My favorite reading naturally tends toward literary fiction, since that is what I like to write. Also, not surprisingly, I like to read about writing. But I also like reading about weird jobs. I like reading about nature (not the "nature is a miracle" genre, more the "gannets produce one egg per year" genre). I like reading about how objects work. I believe that everything I read—from junky murder mysteries to the Bible—feeds my work in ways I cannot fully know.

Next time you're in the library, check out a book that falls far outside your customary tastes. It might spark an idea you would not have stumbled upon otherwise.

Evening was the time for . . .

Rescue a stray key from that junk drawer in the kitchen. Put it next to your word processor or typewriter. Try to remember or imagine what this key once unlocked. Start writing.

A Tip on Dialogue

When writing dialogue, every once in a while allow a character to jump to a conclusion. Conversational leaps add momentum to a scene and force you to get to the main conflict between the characters. The following dialogue is fine, but stuck in a holding pattern:

> Donny opened the door to the landlord.
> "What do you want?"
> "I've got some items to go over with you,"
> Mr. Leadbetter said. "It won't take a minute."
> "It better not."
> Mr. Leadbetter edged into the kitchen. "To be honest, I've had a few complaints about your habits."
> "My habits? Like what?"
> "Like playing music after midnight, things like that. Leaving trash in the hall. That sort of thing."
> "I don't do that. That's Carter in 4B."
> Mr. Leadbetter glanced at his list. "I've also got some complaints about the parrot you keep on the balcony. It scares the neighbors."
> "So what? I signed an ironclad lease."

If you open this same sequence by having Donny jump to a conclusion, in this case a correct one, the scene opens with a little more spark:

> Donny opened the door to the landlord.
> "What do you want?"
> "I've got some items to go over with you," Mr. Leadbetter said. "It won't take a minute."
> "If this is about Junie-Bell's screaming, you can just forget it. There isn't a word in my lease about parrots scaring the neighbors."

Today's horoscope:
Your prized possession
will turn up in
someone else's hands.

"Memory is the way we keep telling ourselves our stories--and telling other people a somewhat different version of our stories. We can hardly manage our lives without a powerful ongoing narrative."

—Alice Munro

Tell a story that most reveals how you see yourself. Are you the hero or the goat? The instigator or the victim? The teller or the told to? Now, turn the story around, casting yourself in the other role. What happens?

Here is my all-time favorite revision exercise: Pick an area of the story or essay that gives you the most trouble. It might be an exchange between two people, a description that is supposed to suggest the psychological heart of the piece— any spot that you don't fully understand yet. Now rewrite it, without peeking at the original, and here's the trick: You may use words of only one syllable.

What I find when doing this exercise is that one-syllable words force me to get to the essence of incident—no fancy stuff. This is pedestrian, basic-food-group writing, and there's nowhere to hide.

Here's another revision tool I began using after discovering the virtues of word processors: Do a Search/Replace on the names of your characters. Make the names rhythmically and aurally as different from the originals as possible. "Alice" becomes "Miranda," "Ben" becomes "Geraldo," and so forth. The resulting draft will take on a mercifully foreign sound, allowing you to review the piece without being hindered by what Annie Dillard calls "the ring of the inevitable." Your piece will no longer have that set-in-stone quality, allowing you a fresher look. When you've finished revising, you can change the names back.

Tempted to quit early?

Make yourself this promise:
One more sentence.

Say this every single time
you want to quit early:

One more sentence.

This is *Bessie*,
an African cape buffalo
from the Prospect Park
Zoo in Brooklyn, who
lived thirty-two years.
Write about the high-
light of Bessie's life.

When I was thirty-three years old,

I wanted nothing more than to publish a book of short stories. I had eight stories in this manuscript, which I sent to contests and mailed to publishers. How I dreaded the sight of my mailbox in the afternoon, the day's mail squashed behind a bulging package—another returned manuscript. But I kept sending it out, because I yearned to publish. The yearning was so intense I often felt sick with it. I had begun writing seriously at twenty-nine, and now, at thirty-three, I was ready to hold a book in my hands and say, "I wrote this." I was a grown-up, old enough to know better, and yet I possessed that stubborn, blind, lazy refusal so common in beginning writers: the refusal to complete our apprenticeship. The refusal to let time enrich our experience, our understanding of craft, our ability to see connections. The refusal to believe that early work is practice work, work that will lead us, if we continue to write, to the real work.

"How do I get published?" the beginning writer—in workshops and classes, at conferences and readings—wants to know. I asked this question myself, long before the question applied. Like so many others in love with writing and words, especially their own words, I wanted to put the cart before the horse—the workhorse, that is.

I am glad now that "success," even in so modest a form, came relatively late to me. I was thirty-seven when I finished my first novel, thirty-nine when it finally came out. Seven more years passed before the publication of my second novel, and now, at this writing, I have another work of fiction in prepublication and another novel that is coming to me inexplicably fast. By the time I'm fifty, I expect I'll have four books of fiction out there. My career feels to me like a very long wait with a sudden burst of activity.

The story collection I was so bent on getting into the world never appeared, thank God. I still have it, though; I admire it as the work of an apprentice, an earnest apprentice working out her craft, her experience, her vision. I forgive her every cliché, every trick ending, every contrivance and shortcut, because I can see she is learning, inching toward what will become her real work. And ten years hence I will forgive her the mistakes she doesn't recognize now.

My friend Bill Roorbach, who writes both fiction and nonfiction beautifully, observes that a writer's apprenticeship usual-ly lasts ten years. That's ten years between the first serious word and the first published word. This pronouncement seems to horrify twenty-year-olds, who have boatloads of time, more than it horrifies forty-year-olds. In any case you'll be ten years older at the end of ten years whether you do an apprenticeship or not, so why not begin?

{ *Respect your apprenticeship.* }

*WRITE ABOUT THE
WORST VISITOR WHO
EVER DARKENED
YOUR DOOR.*

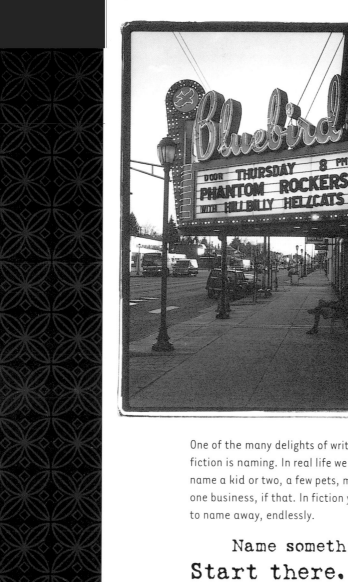

One of the many delights of writing fiction is naming. In real life we get to name a kid or two, a few pets, maybe one business, if that. In fiction you get to name away, endlessly.

Name something.
Start there.

A few years ago

I brought my younger sister on a bird walk with me. She's a vibrant soul, given to extravagance, so I warned her—adequately, I believe—that bird-watching is a quiet pursuit requiring lots of patience and little conversing. Sure, she chirped, ever eager to try something new. I took her to a grove of trees near a pond, and stood there, waiting for some yellowthroats to show up. After about a minute and a half, she said to me: "You mean we have to actually *stand still*?"

I think of this story a lot when meeting people who claim they want to write. You can tell them and tell them how solitary it is, how low on reward, how unsuited to most personalities. But it is only in the doing that they finally understand.

You have to stand still.

TAKE TWO PEOPLE YOU
KNOW WHO SEEM TO BE
OPPOSITES IN EVERY WAY.
THINK ABOUT THEM UNTIL
YOU HIT ON SOMETHING
THEY HAVE IN COMMON.

START WRITING.

Lian Dolan: **So, Tom, none of the "tortured poet" for you?**

Tom Robbins: **Oh, that's a waste of time. That's for amateurs. That's for people who can't get it done on the page, so they have to go out and break up furniture because they can't break up furniture on the page.**

—from the radio program
Satellite Sisters

The myth of the miserable, dissipated writer is just that, a myth. Authentic writers, no matter what their demons, write toward light. Anything else is self-indulgence. The drunken writer is just a drunk who knows how to type. Imagine what he'd accomplish sober. Don't squander your gifts on a bottle or a pipe. Stop posing and start writing. You know who you are.

TODAY'S HOROSCOPE:
A dull person will suddenly become

interesting.

Enter here.

A Few Notes on Theme

Because a couple of my stories have been anthologized in college and high school textbooks, every month or so I get an e-mail from a student. The letter writer is, more often than not, some kid juked on caffeine writing at three in the morning, asking me to "state the themes" of my stories for a term paper that's due on the morrow.

The notion of theme as a separate entity always baffles me. New writers often believe they must begin with a theme, which they too often mistake for a thesis, such as "abortion is bad," "guns should be outlawed," or "people are good at heart." Pity the poor characters who have to follow such leaden sentiments through a preconceived plot. Their chance of making it out of one dimension strikes me as slim indeed.

In fact, theme is something that emerges from a piece— or a series of pieces—after the author has worked the language, the characters, the setting, the plot, and the cadences. Like a sculpture emerging from a hunk of rock, theme resides within an unformed piece but cannot be known until after the creator has been chipping away for a while.

It might occur to you at some point in the process that you're writing about loss and redemption, or the sins of the fathers being visited upon the sons, or something equally grand and abstract, but your characters don't address themselves directly to those things. Neither should you. Reducing any work of art to a "theme" strikes me as absurd, if not hostile.

Write a scene in
which a pair
of shoes figures
prominently.

Juxtaposition

is one hallmark of great story-
telling. Think of big Lenny con-
trasted with his tiny pet mouse
in *Of Mice and Men* or the frigid
winter landscape that provides
the setting for Ethan's brief
inner blooming in *Ethan Frome*.
Juxtaposition, either subtle or
extravagant, infuses even the
quietest stories with dramatic
tension.

Try writing a scene in any
genre in which two seemingly
opposite things go on at the
same time. A French lesson
being offered at the site of an
excavation; a meditative letter
being written at a barn dance;
a lovers' tryst going on at a
wake. Notice how the uneasy fit
between two elements forces
you to imagine differently.

"I feel so often, when I put a book down and say, 'Oh God, I can't keep doing this,' that the book doesn't appear to have been reread, much less rewritten."

—John Irving, from an interview in the *San Francisco Chronicle*

Styptic as he sounds, John Irving exposes a tough truth here. It is so tempting to pronounce our novel, story, poem, essay, or memoir finished before we've done the grunt work.

Is the prose clean and precise? Do the sentences—every single one of them—say what we mean for them to say? Is our command of and respect for language evident in our grammar and usage? Does the punctuation function to clarify our thoughts?

A writer claiming to be no good at grammar is like a carpenter saying he's no good with a hammer. The English language is our one and only tool. It is our obligation and duty to cherish it. And if we shirk this essential duty, we're apt to make readers like John Irving very, very cranky.

Write a
sex scene
and make
it funny.

985003

985003

Every writer needs two critics:

one who gives only praise, and another who never, ever lies. The praiser will be someone who loves you madly: your mother, probably, or your baby brother. The truth-teller should be someone whose taste in literature mirrors yours, who reads widely, who respects you enough to tell you when something's not working.

My praiser is my older sister, Anne, who believes I was a child prodigy and who, from the moment of my first publication, has been shopping for the perfect dress to wear to a Nobel Prize ceremony. Her toughest criticism: "This line isn't quite as stunning and remarkable as the one that precedes it." (I should add, in her defense, that she's a grammar maven with a preternatural ability to catch dangling modifiers.)

My truth-teller is my husband, Dan Abbott, who gets this look—this rueful, grim look—whenever I show him something ill-formed, dishonest, preposterous, or just plain bad. He hates to break the news, but he does anyway.

You know when you need a kick in the seat, and you know when you need an extravagant compliment. Make sure you've got people who can deliver both.

A Tip for Staving Off Writer's Block

Open an encyclopedia to a random page, and read an entry. You might get one good detail (the "sacred ibis" was revered in ancient Egypt) or a whole line of exploration (St. Dunstan's, a British organization that cares for those blinded in war, was founded by a blind newspaper owner) to shake you out of your stupor.

TODAY'S HOROSCOPE: A long-ago mistake comes back to bite you on the backside.

Notes From the Department of Professional Envy

Five minutes after you receive your fifteenth rejection for a novel that took five years to write, a friend—someone you genuinely like and admire—calls with news of a whopping book advance for his first novel. "Wow," you say, stunned, as envy crashes in to slap your face. You feel run over, plowed under, taken utterly by surprise, thinking: Where did this awfulness come from? This smallness? This resentment? I'm not prepared for this!

In fact, you *are* prepared. You—you and nobody else—prepared the place for envy to take up residence in your body and clog the places that should remain open to the imagination, to generosity. Every time you believed yourself a bad writer, envy slithered a little further into your core. Every time a better writer's prose made you feel diminished instead of inspired, envy slipped in. You don't recognize it at the time, have no idea the damage you are doing by resenting your own words as failures instead of stepping-stones to the real stuff. Envy, that snake, slides in and prods you to quit early. It hisses, "Hack! Idiot! Cliché!" as you try to make words into sentences, sentences into paragraphs, paragraphs into something that sings.

There is nothing sudden about envy. The moment of its seemingly theatrical entrance is merely the most recent moment in a continuum. The things you think in that envious moment—*he can write and I can't; he is lucky and I'm not; he has vision and I don't*—follow naturally from all the hissing you've been listening to and taking in without quite hearing it.

Self-doubt is not the opposite of confidence. Envy is the opposite of confidence.

Envy is the thing that says: You will never be lucky. You will never be good. You will never have vision. You will never succeed. You will never have a life like his. Envy serves no purpose except to sap your resources, erode your confidence, and make you bitter when you should be grateful.

Sometimes, though, there is no dismissing it. It is there, in your house, in your room, in your head, in your gut. At these times, allow yourself to surrender, but only for a finite period. Say to yourself: Here's the deal—I get twenty-four hours to not write, to feel rotten, to believe I will never write anything worth reading, ever. After that, get your bony ass back in the chair.

It also helps—it helps me, anyway—to remember that another's success does not equal your failure. Life does not operate on a zero-sum. Another's beautiful prose does not make yours ugly. Another's prize-winning poetry collection does not make yours a prize-losing collection. Another's smart essay does not make yours stupid.

No one else will ever write exactly what you are writing. No one.

If, after this, envy refuses to budge, ask yourself this: Would you really want another life? You can't go around cherry-picking from this life or that one. Maybe you want his Pulitzer, her reviews, his money, her talent, but you'd also have to take his lung X ray, her mother's death, his stutter, her truly hideous hair. And besides, you'd have to give up your singing voice, your friend Robin, the two hundred bird songs you know by ear. So, there you go. Life's a package, and you know—you *know* this—you don't truly want any package but your own.

Usually, the time-limited pity party works. Envy can't get you unless you're feeling vulnerable and inferior, so a day (or a week or a month) away from your work might be just what you need anyway. After a time away, you'll feel grateful for all the words that come, not just the good ones. If envy has any reason at all to exist, that's probably it.

Fill in the blank:

Seven days ago,

_____.

Now, nobody will
talk to me.

"The human animal varies from class to class, culture to culture. In one way we are consistent: We are irrational. Whenever you create a character you must allow for the existence of irrationality."

—Rita Mae Brown, in *Starting From Scratch: A Different Kind of Writers' Manual*

Allow your characters the thrill of surprising you.

My husband once bought a great bottle of wine

that we decided to save until I placed my first short story. This was back when we didn't know up from down about storing wine, and by the time the big day came—four or five years later—the wine had turned. Since then I've made it one of my life missions to celebrate everything. Immediately.

Celebrate if a rejection comes back with a barely discernible "sorry" scrawled in pencil by a human hand. Somebody actually read your work and felt bad about not taking it. *yippee!*

Celebrate when you finish something hard, whether or not it will ever be published. *yessss!*

Celebrate when somebody reads your work and tells you it is good. *Hallelujah!*

When publication finally comes to you, celebrate every part of it: the initial acceptance, the galleys coming in, the editor calling to tell you the publication date, the day you get the final copy in the mail, and on and on.

{ It is possible to live a writing life in a state of perpetual gloom. Don't do it. }

Writing is difficult in lots of ways, but the worst part for me is the occasional bout of boredom. In a long piece especially, my words become dull and predictable and uninspiring because I've read them over too often.

To combat boredom, I sometimes give an old scene a new setting, not because the story needs it, but because I need it, to maintain my interest and at least a small sense of surprise. A scene that has been revised many times gets moved from a kitchen to a backyard or from a school to a church. I'm not making any sweeping alterations here, but the scene feels fresh to me because I have to invent new surroundings.

Words to play with:

fixer

canoodling

blousy

storehouse

ham bone

fink

> "I'm not the sort of writer who can think up great story lines outside of writing. The writing itself is the thing that generates stories for me."
>
> —Alice McDermott, in *Fiction Writer Magazine*

How carefully do you study your own prose? Those early drafts might fall short of your expectations, but the writing itself contains clues to what you're trying to get at.

Combing through an early draft, you might find repeated flight images: bird in the yard, plane overhead, ribbons trailing from a child's pigtails. Is there something brewing in your work that has to do with fleeing or letting go or swooping into foreign matters?

Or, you might find linguistic patterns: many long, looping sentences or many short, sharp ones. What does this syntactical style tell you about the nature of the character? Or the subject? Does a heretofore lighthearted subject take on some weight? Does a serious character possess a hidden cache of whimsy?

You are often your own best repository of ideas—the trick is getting access to all of them on a conscious level.

I have a collection of bird figurines that I keep in my studio. Their presence cheers me, always. I also keep beach rocks, my late uncle's breviary (he was a priest), photographs of dearly departed cats, and a few photos of human loved ones. On the walls I keep art from children I love, a wind chime from a dear old friend, a Felix-the-Cat clock with moving eyes and tail. I also have an amazing doll—a witch clothed in black, with wild hair and black netting for a shawl—that my friend Monty made for me. The witch has long, pointy hands, one of which proffers a cat's-eye marble in the palm. I think of her as the embodiment of my imagination, saying,

"GO AHEAD."

All of these objects inspire me in different ways.

What's in your work space? Do you surround yourself with objects that inspire your work, recall magical times, soothe your mood, buoy your flagging spirits? If not, it's time to take inventory. Make your space compatible with your creative impulses.

This is Marie and Ron. Write about an unlikely friendship.

When a "darning needle" (a scary-looking cross between a dragonfly and a giant mosquito) flew into the kitchen, my six-year-old niece, Anna, worried that she might get stung.

"Oh, they're harmless," I told her. "They just fly around minding their own business."

After a long, worried pause, she said: "What's their business?"

{ Write a dialogue that turns on someone responding in a literal way to a figurative expression. }

"Your most brilliant ideas come in a flash, but the flash comes only after a lot of hard work. Nobody gets a big idea when he is not relaxed, and nobody gets a big idea when he is relaxed all the time."

—Edward Blakeslee

Write about something that is usually fraught with cliché—Christmas, for example—without resorting to a single familiar image. (In other words, no chestnuts roasting on an open fire.)

Strolling through Staples a few years ago,

I happened upon a large whiteboard (also called a dry-erase board) and bought it on a whim. It's the kind that requires those special markers that erase off. After I hung the thing on the wall, it became one of the most indispensable items in my studio.

In fact, I now have two, one large and one small. The small one—about two feet by two feet—is great for keeping idea lists, chapter titles, progress notes, lists of books, and reminders of all kinds. The large one—about three feet by four feet—has room for strategizing longer works. I've put up time lines, family trees, character statistics, and crude maps of imaginary neighborhoods, all of which can be easily erased and revised as the "facts" change.

Using a whiteboard is so much more convenient and soothing than flipping through file folders and random scraps of paper. I also love writing with those markers—it makes me feel so industrious, even if I'm just writing "Freida is thirty-six years old in part one."

{ Get a whiteboard!
It could change your life! }

I met a writer once, an exuberant, unpublished, lovely woman, who described to me her "*genius dance.*" Whenever that moment came, that moment when she realized she'd gotten something exactly, exactly right, she rose from her chair and twirled around, chanting: "*Geeeenuis! Geeeenius!*" I do that now. Really. It amuses me to no end.

{ Remind yourself of your moments of triumph, especially when you're feeling stuck. }

How effective are your details? In many cases, less is more. You don't have to describe a person or thing from top to bottom to give your reader an accurate picture.

First, ask yourself what you want to convey about the thing you are describing. Let's say it's an ostentatious house inhabited by a family whose youngest son is prone to violence. Skip the granite walkway, the wraparound porch, the French doors, the landscaped garden. Rich is rich. Find the one thing in the house that gives away the house's secret:

> "The staircase rose to the upper floors in a theatrical flourish, a swatch of carpet flattened over each tread and tacked hard into the wood."

I like this description because it is so suggestive. The staircase seems to belong to a house big enough and nice enough to have "upper floors," and yet there's a weird sense of menace to those flattened carpet swatches and the way they're attached to the treads.

*Describe a wedding in which nothing
—absolutely nothing—
goes wrong. Add a character who hates perfection.*

Writing requires discipline, but disciplined writers are not necessarily prolific. Most good work gets produced over time, sometimes many years, allowing the writer to grow with the material, to allow his world, his command over craft, and his psychological maturity to coalesce at just the right moment to produce something of value. This process often involves dreadful periods of not writing, or, worse, periods of writing very badly, embarrassingly badly. As time passes in a writing life, the writer learns not to fear these arid periods. The words come back eventually. That's the real discipline: to train the mind and heart into believing that words come back.

I can think of a handful of writers who are both prolific *and* good: Joyce Carol Oates, Madison Smartt Bell, Anne Tyler. There is a certain genius at work in these cases, though; the rest of us normal writers have to suffer the droughts and hope for rain.

Be willing to wait. In the meantime, write when you don't feel like it. If you can't write, read.

FINISH THE FOLLOWING SENTENCE IN THE VOICE OF SOMEONE TEN YEARS OLDER OR TEN YEARS YOUNGER THAN YOU:

THE ONLY THING I EVER WANTED WAS

_____.

Remember Mr. Potato Head? I loved the guy! I loved applying all those brightly colored, plastic accoutrements: the top hat, the big red lips, the bow tie, the different ears and noses.

Don't write stories that are so plot-driven that your characters appear to have events worked upon them by an unseen hand. Stories in which a character never acts, but is only acted upon. Stories in which one-dimensional characters walk through a preordained plot, where their only function is to play out your notions or prove your point.

{ Don't write a Mr. Potato Head story. }

Your character is being followed.

Imagine a coat.

Imagine the pocket of the coat.

Imagine what's in the pocket.

Children love to be surprised.

Write something for a child in

which an animal works against type:

an unwise owl,

a disloyal dog,

a needy cat,

a slow rabbit,

a fast turtle.

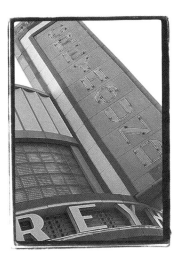

Five Writing Ideas That Take a Little Nerve

❶ Buy a round-trip bus ticket to anywhere, and write on the bus.

❷ Go to the introductory meeting of something that fascinates you —a Dale Carnegie seminar, for example, or a Crimewatch group.

❸ Hang out in a train station for a few hours, asking people where they're coming from or where they're going.

❹ Call a temp agency, and take the first short-term job they offer you.

❺ Sneak into a lecture at a college, university, tech school, or training institute, and take notes.

"I was worried about the book's ending while I was writing, but I told myself to have faith, and that if I stayed true to the characters, the story would finish itself."

—Elizabeth Strout, from an interview in iVillage.com

There comes a point in any long piece of writing—and even in some short ones—when the writer loses faith in her ability to unwind the ball of yarn that has taken so long to tangle up in just the right way. Don't quit on yourself. You might need a few weeks away from the piece to gain better perspective, but the solution exists somewhere in your subconscious. Faith is exactly the right word for what you need right now.

{ Keep going. }

Write a scene in which the dramatic tension revolves around a misspelling: a road sign, the name on a birthday cake, the directions to a doctor's office, a word in a spelling bee . . .

TODAY'S HOROSCOPE: A VERY SMALL PROBLEM FOR YOU WILL BECOME A VERY BIG PROBLEM FOR SOMEONE ELSE.

"Try to leave out the part that readers tend to skip."

—advice to writers from Elmore Leonard, in *The New York Times*

Elmore Leonard is speaking here of the parts we love to write, the long description of our first apartment or the tornado we saw once in Missouri or the adorable way our ancient dog, Baskerville, used to pretend to kill woodchucks by digging up old ones (well, all right, maybe we wouldn't skip that). But you get the idea. At some point after your first, headlong draft, you have to figure out which parts are in there not because the reader or the story requires them, but because (choose one):

❶ you're fresh out of a writing program and would like to demonstrate your literary chops;
❷ you're working out stupendous psychological problems and writing is cheaper than therapy;
❸ you're trying to fatten up a thin story with a bunch of extra words.

We could all add our own line to this list. Let's take Elmore's advice instead.

{ Safe }

A Note From the Department of Solitary Confinement

Once every six weeks or so, I attend a "salon," a highfalutin name my low-falutin friends have given to a gathering of artists who eat, drink, gossip, talk shop, and share work. The only thing we require of each other is applause. It's a great time to shed the inner critic, seek out conviviality, and feel like a real artist.

Write about **TROUBLE**
resulting from a good deed.

A Tip on Style

Colors can be delivered as similes that suggest something about the character's inner life. Your reader will receive a character in a red shirt a little differently if that shirt is described as the color of spilled wine or fresh liver or SpaghettiOs. A person's skin can be the color of dead leaves or dust or mud or newborn mice or cocoa or cantaloupe or cream or plums or maize . . .

Ten Commandments for a Happy Writing Life

❶ Don't wait for inspiration; establish a writing habit.

❷ Take time off.

❸ Read voraciously.

❹ Shut out the inner critic.

❺ Claim a space.

❻ Claim some time.

❼ Accept rejection.

❽ Expect success.

❾ Live fully.

❿ Wish others well.

At some point in any writing life, the writer has to decide what to do about rejection. Some people save rejection slips and laugh about using them to wallpaper the bathroom. Others get two or three rejections and quit. Most aspiring writers assume that rejection is a phase of the writing life that one simply gets through, after which success comes easily and rejection comes rarely, if at all. Boy, oh boy. In truth, rejection is part of every writing life, even the ones you would never suspect.

When I was a beginning writer, I attended a fiction reading by the short-story master, Andre Dubus, now deceased but still a major influence on writers both young and old. He read a story that quieted the room, then, in the Q and A afterward, mentioned that the *Sewanee Review* had just rejected it. I sat there, astounded and grateful, almost unable to believe that a writer of this caliber got those little slips in the mail, too. It was a turning-point moment in my writing life that I will never forget.

I stopped saving rejection slips after that. I had deluded myself into thinking that keeping my stash made me brave and cocky, but in truth I saved rejections to remind myself that I wasn't very good yet, that I wasn't really a writer. Why I did that, I don't fully know, but I do know that those printed slips lost their power over me after Andre Dubus invoked them at that reading.

They're just pieces of paper.
Let go.

TODAY'S HOROSCOPE: Something **big** is brewing **behin**d your **b**a**c**k.

TODAY'S HOROSCOPE

SOMEBODY CLOSE TO
YOU WILL TELL YOUR
secret.

Almost any situation includes insiders and outsiders.
Most human beings, no matter what their stations,
consider themselves outsiders.

{ Write about being an insider. }

Create a set of circumstances in which a reasonable person would indeed cry over spilled milk.

"I've been married for twenty-
five years, and I drive a four-
door sedan around town, and
try to pay the bills on time. My
characters are much, much more
interesting than I am."

—Charles Baxter, talking about *The Feast of Love*

Are your characters too much like you? Have a
little fun, for crying out loud! Mix things up a little:
Give your darlings an inherited flea circus, a mother-
in-law who trains snakes, a daughter who hears
voices. Move out of your neighborhood, and take a
walk on the wild side. If you already live on the wild
side, put the gun away and try your hand at canasta.

Writers should understand the rules of grammar, usage, punctuation, form, and structure.

Once you've learned the rules—once you really, really know what you're doing with the English language—have a party: Tell a story backwards. Write a poem in which the beginning words, not the end words, rhyme. Write an opinion piece in the second person. Have a little fun.

{ Break a rule. }

Write about a long,
fraught ride in a car.

✳ ✳ ✳ ✳

"What put me over the top was that [*The New York Times* book critic] Michiko Kakutani gave my last novel such a scathing review, and it had such a bad fallout—I mean just terrible, not just psychologically for me, which it did, but across the board in terms of killing the book. I'm just not going to do it anymore. If I have any advance warning, I'm simply not going to read these things . . . It sounds kind of churlish to say I don't read bad reviews—it sounds defensive and unsophisticated—but after Kakutani's review of *Dara Falcon,* I figured it isn't worth doing this to myself."

—Ann Beattie, in an interview with Chris Wright in the *Boston Phoenix*

This raw admission surprised me when I read it. I couldn't imagine a writer as accomplished as Ann Beattie chafing over a bad review, and yet she clearly felt stung by that rebuke from the *Times* and sobered by what it did to the life of a book she clearly believed in. The lesson here is that criticism hurts, no matter who you are. And if you're a writer, the criticism is going to be public in a way you can't afford to imagine while you're in the throes of creating the very thing you plan to lay at the public's feet.

If you can't afford to imagine disapprobation, then at some point the only solution is not to face it. I know of many writers who, after a few years and a couple of books, stop reading reviews altogether. We all have that inner critic who likes to mess with our confidence; when that inner critic becomes flesh and blood, it's all over but the cryin'.

Now, maybe your critics aren't the likes of Michiko Kakutani—yet. But is there anyone else who has stung you in the same way? Your mother? A teacher? Your girlfriend? Take some advice from Ann Beattie: Stop listening.

Before you batten down the hatches, though, be sure to remember the important distinction between useful criticism for works in progress and rebuke of the finished product. Most of us need feedback at certain points during the writing process; don't reject that useful step even if it occasionally causes pain or even embarrassment. If you have any judgment at all, you can tell the difference between those who mean to help you and those who don't. Cherish the former, and get rid of the latter.

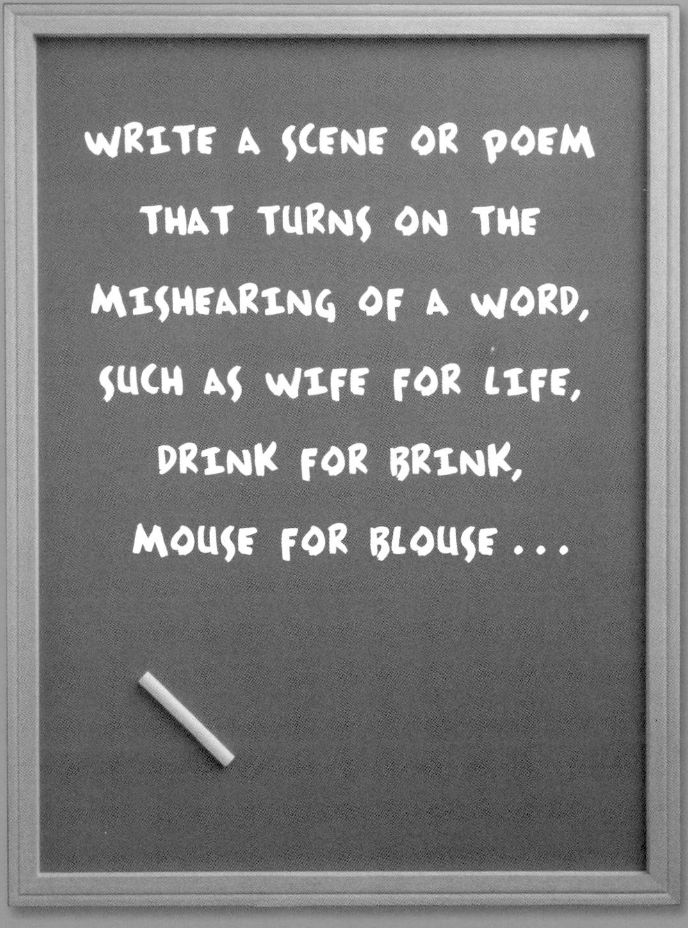

WRITE A SCENE OR POEM
THAT TURNS ON THE
MISHEARING OF A WORD,
SUCH AS WIFE FOR LIFE,
DRINK FOR BRINK,
MOUSE FOR BLOUSE...

Stuck in mid-draft?

Try changing the point of view, even for a few paragraphs, to see what moves.

Of her novel *Bel Canto*, which follows a terrorist takeover at the home of a South American vice president, Ann Patchett says, "I wanted to find a way to grieve for something I had read about in the paper."

Find something in the paper today worth grieving. Don't pick the obvious stories, the head-line-grabbers about mothers drowning their children. Instead, find some quietly horrifying story, a page-five story that almost no one else will read carefully. The obituaries usually include an unmourned soul worth a spin or two of your imagination.

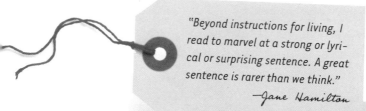

"Beyond instructions for living, I read to marvel at a strong or lyrical or surprising sentence. A great sentence is rarer than we think."

—Jane Hamilton

Set a deceptively small goal for today:

One great sentence.

I have known many writers who have worked on a single piece of writing for years. I mean *years*. Usually it's a novel, but sometimes it's a memoir or a family story or a long poem or essay. They work and work and work, take months off to feel discouraged and blocked, and then turn back to the same work, which now feels heavy and stale. And yet, on they plow.

Part of me admires this kind of doggedness; another part of me wonders how on earth these people manage to get up in the morning. I write fiction. But I write different kinds of fiction—stories, novels, connected stories. I also write articles on writing, book reviews, books for high school teachers who teach fiction, and books like this one, for fellow writers. Every once in a while I write a short essay. If I didn't have these varying ways of approaching my writing day, and my life, I'd be hiding in bed with the covers over my face.

I wonder sometimes if the one-story obsession is a perverted form of writer's block. If the writer writes only one thing, and that one thing never gets finished, then she will never have to be judged on her work and she will never have to write anything else.

{ Don't be afraid. Try something else.
You do have more than one story. }

"I don't like people to talk for no reason, but I really like dialogue between people who aren't listening to each other."

--Raymond Carver

Write a passage of dialogue between
two people at cross purposes.

Fill in the blank, and then keep going:

Until _____, nothing notable
had happened in the town of Madison
since the year of its founding.

Notes From the Department of Intestinal Fortitude

How much are you willing to throw away? I believe, deeply, that until a writer is willing to throw away not only the bad stuff, but the good stuff that is merely good in itself but not good for the whole, he is not fully matured as a writer.

It hurts to throw out words, lines, sentences, paragraphs, stanzas, chapters, whole damn books. I know it hurts because I've done it, over and over. Every writer does. It stops hurting after a while because the reward—the beautiful reward—is liberation from your own gifts. I once worked on a story unsuccessfully for many months because I could not bear to throw away the first line, which anchored the story to a path the story did not wish to take. Finally I ditched that line, which I do not now remember, and it was like letting the air out of a balloon—in a good way. That story zigged and zagged, thrilled to be let go of. I followed its wild course, happened in due time upon the right one, and eventually found that story a good home.

The first line, which I did not save, was a lovely line, I am sure. Good riddance.

Just for today, write in an unaccustomed place.
A café, a park bench, a carrel in the local library.
What happens?

Write about an ordinary ritual
in which something goes

terribly wrong.

"I've always been interested in writing about people . . .

who are not able to speak for themselves. As in my

novel *Black Water*—I provide a voice for someone who

has died and can't speak for herself."

—Joyce Carol Oates

{ Write something in the voice of someone
who has, until now, been silent. }

Just for today, try writing at an unaccustomed time. Night owls can fire up the coffeepot and get cracking by dawn; morning folks can investigate the wee hours, just to see what happens.

Describe the longest, happiest, or most excruciating hour of your life without using abstractions such *as fear, death, love, happy, upset, confused*. Instead, infuse the piece with concrete words such as *chair, coffee, chartreuse, crooked, flavor, sand, shingles, crack*. Avoid words like *pain*, and embrace words like *pane*. If you can't see it, smell it, touch it, taste it, or hear it, give it the old heave-ho. Notice how vivid the writing becomes when you force feelings to take concrete forms.

Who were your parents when they were your age?

Readers want to like the main character. If your main character is not likeable, then at the very least, he should be understandable. There should be an underlying logic to his bad behavior, twisted though that logic might be. With this in mind, write about someone who profits from a tragedy.

Write a scene that
turns on a ransom
note—for something
other than a
human being.

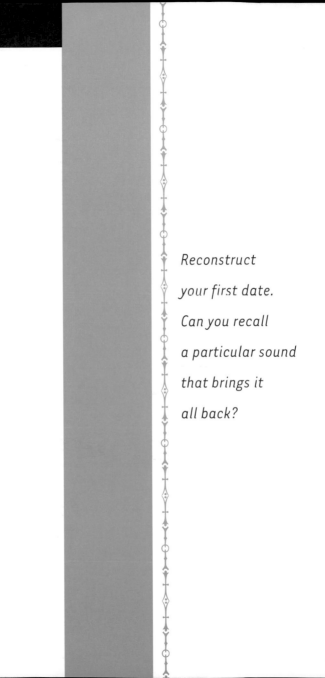

*Reconstruct
your first date.
Can you recall
a particular sound
that brings it
all back?*

Write about
the last time
you felt
indispensable.

"I'm interested in people who find themselves in places, either of their choosing or not, and who are forced to decide how best to live there. That feeling of both citizenship and exile, of always being an expatriate—with all the attendant problems and complications and delight."

— Chang-rae Lee, in an interview with
Dwight Garner in *The New York Times*

Think of a mismatch between a person and a place. It may be someone in the wrong house, the wrong job, the wrong school, the wrong political party, the wrong club, the wrong choir, the wrong . . .

A Note From the
Department of Attitude Adjustment

I was sitting at a table in a Barnes & Noble
with a stack of my novels at my elbow, wish-
ing to be anywhere but here, in this city
where nobody knew me and where not a soul
in sight appeared remotely interested in
buying my book. An elderly woman happened
by, leaned on her cane, and gushed: "This
must be the culmination of all your hopes
and dreams!"

  First, I laughed, thinking she must be a
writer, too, familiar with the humiliations
of the road. But she was serious and contin-
ued to gaze at me with unabashed awe.
Finally, just to be polite, I said, "Yes, it
is." After she left (she did buy a book), I
began to think: She's right. This is the culmination of all my hopes and dreams. I get
to do the thing I love most, only the small-
est part of which is less than joyful. I
think of that woman often. I thank her.

This week, tell everyone you know
that you're out of town. Send the kids
to Aunt Rosie's; kennel the dogs;
stock up on takeout; unplug the television; don't touch the e-mail; and do
not answer the phone. Have yourself
a one-person artists' colony experience. You will never be the same.

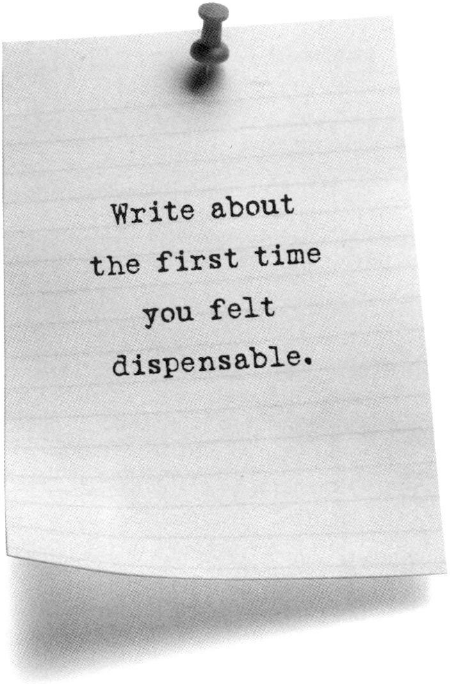

Write about
the first time
you felt
dispensable.

MOST GOOD STORIES ARE ABOUT TROUBLE.

Trouble getting from point A to point B
Trouble being understood
Trouble understanding
Trouble doing something
Trouble having something done to you
Trouble talking
Trouble listening
Trouble within
Trouble without
Trouble being human

The list is endless, of course. When your own
work befuddles you, ask yourself: What is the
nature of the trouble I am trying to explore?

To take stock of your writing life,

begin small. What does Monday usually look like? Is there some small adjustment you can make—a different starting time for work, a train ride instead of a car ride, a longer lunch break, a stand-in to pick up the kids—that will allow you a half hour of writing time that you don't normally get? Like everything else in your life, writing time is something you have to schedule. Sure, it's antiromantic, but it's the only way you're going to get that book finished—or started.

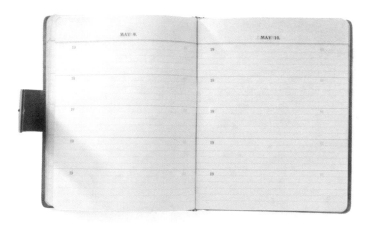

Read your work aloud. It's amazing how much more easily you'll zero in on the unlovely word, the awkward phrase, the faulty thinking.

Another hummingbird fact writers can relate to: twenty percent of its body weight is *heart.*

During the first draft of anything I write, whether it's a short article or a novel, I find myself getting up and down continually, almost as if the work were too bright to look at directly. I used to consider this approach to the blank page a flaw in my character, but I have come to refer to it affectionately as the Hummingbird Method of Writing.

Hummingbirds approach flowers in much the way I approach a first draft: sip, draw back, sip, draw back, sip, draw back. They seem to eat practically nothing, and yet this herky-jerky method nets them half their body weight in nectar in a single day.

I also like hummingbirds because they hibernate—really. In hostile conditions they can enter a torpor, their breathing nearly indiscernible, their reactions either very slow or entirely lacking. Sound familiar?

*Write about your
earliest superstition.*

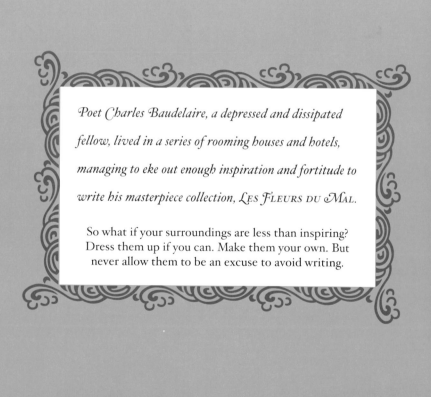

Poet Charles Baudelaire, a depressed and dissipated
fellow, lived in a series of rooming houses and hotels,
managing to eke out enough inspiration and fortitude to
write his masterpiece collection, LES FLEURS DU MAL.

So what if your surroundings are less than inspiring?
Dress them up if you can. Make them your own. But
never allow them to be an excuse to avoid writing.

Write about an
escalating dispute
between two normally
polite, upstanding
neighbors. How do
they manifest
**resentment,
rage, revenge?**

This is *Judy,*
who is having her toenails inspected.
Write about two creatures--human or
animal--whose sense of power is
altered by each other's presence.

"For whatever is truly wondrous and fearful in man, never yet was put into words or books."

—Herman Melville

There is always something new to say. Say it.

> "Get your facts first, and then you can distort them as much as you please."
>
> —Mark Twain

I once shadowed my veterinarian, a sweet man named Tom Aylers, over the course of a typical work day. I'm always on the lookout for inside info on people's jobs, since my characters tend to play out their dramas while working. I've created receptionists, flight attendants, hairdressers, nuns, pipefitters, flower shop owners, and paper mill managers, though I've never once done any of these jobs for even a day. What I do is talk to people, and I've found that most folks love to talk about what they do.

My day at the veterinary hospital turned out to be so draining that it was a year before I used any of the material. Following Dr. Aylers and his colleague, Dr. Smith, I bore witness to a seemingly endless demonstration of heartache. They euthanized Hershal, an old black dog with a white muzzle who stared at me from his cage, waiting for his owners to come in and say good-bye. They operated on an orange cat named Clancy who turned out to have a hopeless cancer. At the end of the day a weeping young couple came in with a golden retriever in their arms—and carried its body out a few minutes later to bury in their backyard. Dr. Aylers assured me that an average day did not normally accommodate so much death, but I cried on the way home anyway.

When I finally got around to using my research—I filled up two tapes and many pages of a steno pad—I used almost none of it. I had plenty of facts and figures, but what I really needed, and got, from my meager research was just enough of a grounding to start making things up. Research, for fiction writers, is funny that way; we require lots and lots of information in order to put down one or two sentences that ring with authority.

Follow someone for a day or two, until you feel brave enough to reinvent the experience.

A postscript: The story with the vet in it was one I liked and my editor didn't, so it got cut from the final version of the book. I owe my vets an apology. Here it is.

A Tip on Revision

In revision the tiniest adjustments make a difference. For instance, how closely do you attend to the placement of dialogue tags? Placement can change the rhythm of a line and also its meaning.

> "I saw Sally at the Goldsteins' this morning," Byron said.

> "I saw Sally at the Goldsteins'," Byron said. "This morning."

In the second example, Byron seems to imply that Sally wasn't supposed to be at the Goldsteins'—the pause before "this morning" loads the phrase with suggestion. Maybe Sally was at the Goldsteins' after telling her husband she was going to work. Maybe Sally goes to the Goldsteins' a lot, but never in the morning. Maybe Sally has been banned from the Goldsteins' after killing their dog or cutting down their flagpole.

Write about the first time
you truly understood that
all life ends in death.

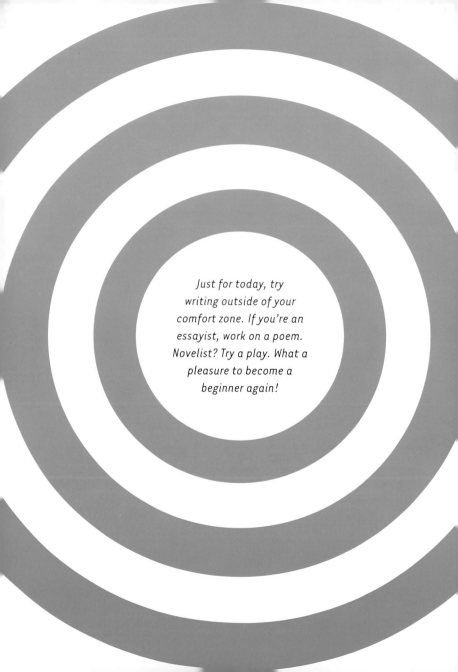

Just for today, try writing outside of your comfort zone. If you're an essayist, work on a poem. Novelist? Try a play. What a pleasure to become a beginner again!

Try these in a paragraph: homeland

flummoxed

uncles

fanfare

last rites

tomcat

What is the longest time you ever waited for someone or something?
Why did you wait?

Every October my friend Amy invites me and several other artists to her family camp in New Hampshire for a three-day retreat. We bring our supplies (art or writing), work all day (with time out for a swim or walk), then join up in the evening for food, wine, a sunset, and an easy conversation. We've been doing this for about six years, and I've since discovered that many writers I know (most of them women, actually) have the same sort of thing going with their friends.

{ Look around you: Can you recruit your intimates to begin a similar tradition? }

The world contains winners and losers.
Most of us identify with the losers.

Write about being a winner.

Write about a person who wins something she does not want.

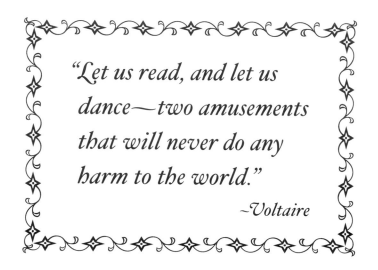

"Let us read, and let us dance—two amusements that will never do any harm to the world."

~Voltaire

Don't write to hurt. Understand that a line exists between your story and somebody else's privacy. This line is zigzaggy at best, and it takes a clear eye to follow its path. Writers have the right to write. We know this. But there's a difference between writing to purge and writing to illuminate.

I have known a couple of people who wrote for revenge; as far as I can tell, publication didn't make them feel any better. Of course the worst part is that vengeful writing usually isn't good; that's what personal journals are for, to collect that bad, small, narrow-eyed writing and keep it private.

If you are embarking on a piece of writing you believe you'll have to shield from certain readers—a family member, a former friend, an erstwhile lover—think it through before beginning. My advice is to wait six months. There are so many other things to write! If in six months the story is still lodged within your gut, that's probably a sign that the story needs writing. But be careful.

FINISH THIS LINE IN A VOICE
OTHER THAN YOUR OWN:

RIGHT AFTER THEY POSTED
THE RESULTS, I TRIED TO

_____

_____.

A Tip on Style

One way to intensify a description is to allow style to work against content. For example, you might describe a bucolic farm in the vernacular of the urban: fence posts lined up like cops at a riot or a silo's noonday glinting reminiscent of a brandished gun.

Today's horoscope:
Unwanted information comes to
you through a surprising channel.

When stuck or bored with your work,
try making up titles.

"The Sturgeon"
"Six Mirrors"
"The Piano Movers"
"A Fine Woman Looks for Rain"
"Did You Hear That?"

You could do this all day just for your own
amusement, but this little exercise often
sparks an idea. The worst than can hap-
pen is that you'll get tired of fooling
around and eventually get back to work.

"Free Lunch: A Fable"

"The Longest Day"

"Clap, Clap, Bow"

"Why Millie Gardenia
Broke Our Windows"

> "I think writer's block is simply the dread that you are going to write something horrible."
>
> —Roy Blount, Jr.

Nobody has to see that first draft but you. You can eat it when you're done. You can make it into origami animals and decorate a table. You can dunk it in hot water, stir it up, mash it back into pulp. You can build a fire, line a birdcage, stuff a pillow.

You can't do any of this, however, until you write the thing.

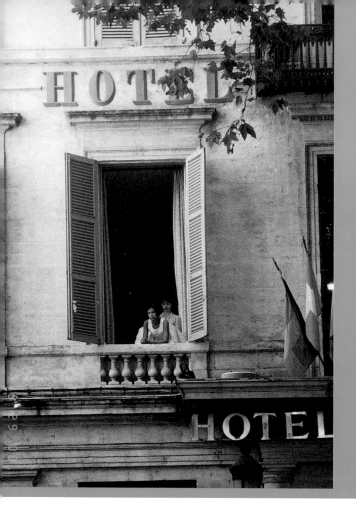

My friend Alison, who has four kids, rented
a motel room for three days just to write.
She claims it changed her life.

Get out of town.

Write about a grown-up
who does not play well
with others.

This morning I was sitting
in a bakery listening to
two very old men.
Here is a verbatim snippet
of their conversation:

> "How are you, Ben?
> I don't mean health-wise.
> I mean spirit-wise."

> "Well, I got my hair cut
> yesterday."

I assume that Ben meant
he was feeling just dandy,
spirit-wise.

> { Let your characters respond indirectly.
> Imagine all the ways there are to say
> "yes" or "no" or "fine, thank you." }

What is the subject you're avoiding?
Write it down.

That's all for now.
Tomorrow maybe you'll be
able to get a sentence out,
and then a paragraph.

Diminished

Invent a circumstance in which a character is forced to change his name.

Someone has left a note on a car windshield.

Begin with a character at odds with his or her
physical environment. She has a broken foot,
and the elevator doesn't work. He arrives at
the beach house with the wrong set of keys.

Escalate the conflict by adding a second
character who is more hindrance than help.

Make your characters more than they are.
If you're going to jump, jump off a cliff, not a chair

Write about your hidden talent.

There is nothing like a deadline to get the Muse off her backside. If you don't have a deadline, then create one and get somebody to hold you to it. Make it reasonable but not too easy.

Start writing.

Seven Rules of Etiquette for Giving a Reading

❶ Arrive on time, even if you're famous.

❷ If you're reading poems, don't explain them first. If you must add an intro, don't make it longer than the poem.

❸ Select something that reads well *aloud,* which might not be your very best work. Dialogue reads well, as do passages containing some humor. If the work is dark and humorless, pick a piece with good pacing and a bit of suspense.

❹ Don't hug the lectern or hide your face in the pages. The last thing you want from the audience is pity. Even if you're sick with anxiety, stand up straight.

❺ Slow down. Most people read too fast.

❻ Don't read longer than thirty to forty minutes. People will get restless, no matter how good you are. If you're on with more than one other reader, limit yourself to fifteen minutes. Time yourself beforehand—it always takes longer than you think.

❼ If you faint during the reading (I know someone who did this), fall into a coughing jag, or otherwise disgrace yourself, don't belabor it afterward. Just smile and say thanks to the good souls who compliment you. The next time will go better.

Write a piece — fiction
or nonfiction, poetry,
or script — in which
three objects exist at
the beginning and only
one at the end.

A man and woman, unrelated, are trying
to get a child down from a tree.

"It is the deepest desire of every writer, the one we never admit or even dare to speak of: to write a book we can leave as a legacy. And although it is sometimes easy to forget, wanting to be a writer is not about reviews or advances or how many copies are printed or sold. It is much simpler than that, and much more passionate. If you do it right, and if they publish it, you may actually leave something behind that can last forever."

—Alice Hoffman,
from *The New York Times*

Don't forget to be grateful that you love words.